Two Master Magicians: Robert-Houdin and Houdini

by Alicia Morton

PEARSON

Glenview, Illinois • Boston, Massachusetts • Chandler, Arizona
Upper Saddle River, New Jersey

Wonder

Harry Houdini became a famous magician. When he was a child, he loved magic shows. He wanted to know how magicians did their tricks.

Houdini read books. One book was by a famous magician. His name was Jean-Eugène Robert-Houdin. Robert-Houdin died before Houdini was born. He was important to Houdini.

Jean-Eugène Robert-Houdin

Harry Houdini

Robert-Houdin was a magician from France. He was called "The Father of Modern Magic." Houdini liked him very much. Houdini even used part of Robert-Houdin's name.

Houdini's real name was Ehrich Weisz. He was born in Hungary in 1874. He made his new name by adding an *i* to *Houdin*.

Houdini became famous for his great escapes.

Masters and Magic

Robert-Houdin and Houdini both became master magicians. They did it in different ways. One thing was the same. They made up new tricks.

Robert-Houdin

Robert-Houdin learned magic tricks when he was young. He read a book about tricks. He practiced the tricks. He worked hard. His hands moved quickly. People could not see how he did the tricks.

Robert-Houdin became a stage magician at age 40.

Magicians trick you. They make you look at something. Then you do not watch the trick. You cannot see how it happens.

The Disappearing Person Trick

Robert-Houdin made a person "disappear." The trick worked like this:
- His helper stood close to the screen. People could not see the screen.
- Robert-Houdin twirled his cape in front of his helper.
- The helper quickly stepped behind the screen.
- Robert-Houdin dropped the cape. The helper was gone! People thought the helper had disappeared.

Houdini

When he was young, Houdini had to quit school. His family was poor. He had to work to help them.

One night, Houdini bought a book. It was about Robert-Houdin.

Houdini was tired of working. He hoped he could make money doing magic tricks. He learned more about magic from Robert-Houdin's book.

Houdini was inside this box in 1914. It was put in the water. He escaped in two minutes and 55 seconds!

Houdini became famous for his escapes. He learned about locks. He learned how to get out of locked boxes. Sometimes he asked the police to lock him in jail. He escaped every time.

He also learned to hold his breath. He got used to very cold water. These things were important for a big trick. Houdini was chained up. Then he was put in a locked box. The box was put in icy water. He escaped!

Wonderful Tricks

Both men did great tricks. They made magic in different ways.

Robert-Houdin used science in his tricks. He was the first to do this. He made his tricks seem easy.

Houdini did exciting tricks. He trained his body to be strong. He made his escapes look hard. But he was just pretending.

Now you know about these magicians. Which trick do you like best?